Then AND Now

Then AND Now

THE LIFE STORY OF
BONNIE BAKER

BONNIE BAKER

Christian Living Books, Inc.
An imprint of Pneuma Life Publishing
Largo, MD

ISBN 1-56229-010-X

Printed in the United States of America

Unless otherwise marked, all Scripture quotations are taken from the King James Version of the Bible.

Christian Living Books, Inc.
An imprint of Pneuma Life Publishing, Inc.
P.O. Box 7584
Largo, MD 20792
301-218-9092
www.christianlivingbooks.com

Author Contact
P.O. Box 74073
Romulus, MI 48174-0073

$\mathscr{D}$EDICATION

I dedicate this book to my husband, Willie, and to my daughters, Tawana, Kenyatta, Chantel and LaChisa, for their love, understanding and support during the many hours I spent writing this book; to my editors; and to the Spirit of the Lord for inspiring me to write.

Contents

FOREWORD

For such a time as this, God has allowed Evangelist Bonnie Baker to write her life story. This book is a must for many in the body of Christ who are struggling with their past. *Then and Now* reveals the awesome delivering power of God through steadfast intercessory prayer. Evangelist Baker is a perfect example of 2 Corinthians 5:17, which states, *"Therefore if any man be in Christ, he is a new creature: old things are passed away; behold, all things are become new."*

As many people read this book, they will be delivered and set free. Unanswered questions will be answered, and many will be better equipped to handle the adversity that is to come. The light will be shed on the truth because, according to John 8:36, *"If the son therefore shall make you free, ye shall be free indeed."*

I have had the privilege of knowing Bonnie Baker personally. I walked with her sister as she stood in the gap and travailed until God brought forth deliverance. There remains no residue of Evangelist Baker's past in her.

God has released her to reveal the tricks of the enemy and how to recognize his lies so God's people can walk in total victory. This book also reveals how God has a purpose and a plan for our lives, and how when a person is totally sold out to God, He can use him or her in a mighty way.

I believe that as you read this book and obey God's Word, He will bless you as He has Bonnie Baker. It's stated in Deuteronomy 28:13: *"And the Lord shall make thee the head, and not the tail; and thou shalt be above only, and thou shalt not be beneath; if that thou hearken unto the commandments of the Lord thy God, which I command thee this day, to observe and to do them."*

Pastor Dorothy Hyman
Fountain of Praise
Queens, New York

$\mathscr{P}$REFACE

Often the Spirit of the Lord will save and raise up a certain, unknown woman or man, someone who is not in every bookstore or on every bookshelf, someone who is not in the marketplace. The Spirit will do this so God can get ALL the glory (as in The New Testament) with a testimony that has the ability and power to go into the spirit and bring deliverance, victory and salvation to the multitudes.

Such is the case with this woman of God, a woman who has paid the price and dedicated her life to the work of the Lord. She has traveled the world ministering in churches, preaching, teaching and sharing her life stories to bring deliverance to thousands for the glory of the Lord Jesus Christ.

Bonnie Baker will capture your attention in such a way that you will find new hope to believe and trust the Lord when it comes to your loved ones. You will realize that nothing is impossible with God if you don't give up, you continue to trust the timing of the Lord, and you lean not on your own understanding but lean and depend on His lead.

As you read this book, you will laugh, cry and pray as you see the power of the Lord set free and mold this vessel. You will see Bonnie Baker's life as it was, torn and broken, bring her face to face with the living God of Israel to begin the metamorphosis of her life into a new person, a vessel of honor fit for the master's use and glory.

I encourage you to be bold and believe God for your loved ones and know that difficulties shall come to pass. He loves you and wants you to have household salvation.

Your co-laborer in the Gospel and biological sister,
Evangelist Hattie White
First Lady, Redeeming the Time Ministry
Greenville, North Carolina

$\mathscr{A}$CKNOWLEDGMENTS

First, I would like to thank God my Father, my Lord and my Savior, Jesus Christ and His Holy Spirit for inspiring me to write this book. I'd like to thank my very best friend, my beloved and dear husband whom I love, Willie Dean Baker, for all of his love, support and encouragement.

I'd also like to thank my four daughters, Tawana, Kenyatta, Chantel and LaChisa, and my spiritual daughter, Chrissy. Kenyatta, I especially thank you for the numerous glasses of water you brought to me during the many hours I sat at the table writing.

To my dad and mom, who are in heaven, thank you for the love you gave me while molding me into the best and helping me to become the lady God planned for me to be. I love you.

To my three sons and six daughters who are in heaven, Mommy loves you.

I would like to say a special thank you to my sweet sister and brother-in-law, Pastor Lonnie White and First Lady Hattie White, for praying me through on numerous occasions, for loving me, being there for me, helping me in my time of need and encouraging me all the time. I love you both.

A special thanks to my brother-in-law and sister-in-law, Ron and Doris Baker, and especially to Doris for helping me with the typing and editing of this book and working with me for many hours. I love you.

To my entire family, including nieces and nephews, I love you. To Pastor Dorothy Hyman, Deacon Hyman and the Fountain of Praise church family in Queens, New York, thank you for all your support and love. I love you. I would like to thank God for the memory of my deceased pastor, Apostle Charles O. Miles. Especially in my early years of salvation, he provided guidance, prayers, support and encouragement during my spiritual journey.

Thanks also go to Dr. Luvenia Miles for all her prayers, love and support. To my beloved Pastor, Marvin N. Miles, and First Lady Carolyn L. Miles, thanks for all the love, encouragement and support you've given me to write this book. I love you.

To Mother Mildred Poole, thanks for being there for me, taking me under your wings, and nourishing and loving me for who I am. To my new mother, Mary Jordan-Meeks, thank you for your love, prayers and support. I love you.

To all my godchildren, I love you. To Elder Robert and Sister Eazelle Hodges, thanks for being true friends through the years. Thanks for your spiritual encouragement and love. I love you.

To my friend Nikkie, thank you for being there and helping me with the girls so many times, too many to mention. I love you.

To my best friend, Marlene, thank you for all your love and support. I love you.

To Gloria, I love you and thank you for praying, encouraging and supporting me.

To a special friend, Lecie, thank you for all your love and support and for being a great neighbor. Thanks for being there.

To my IGC family, thank you all. I love you. To Mrs. Winn at Jireh Financial, thank you for your encouragement and introduction to the mortgage world. May God continue to bless you. To Marc King at Complete Mortgage, thank you for your support and love. To Sis. Gladney, thank you for all the love and support. I would also like to personally thank Kimberly and Christian Living Books for all the editing, hours of support, love and many phone calls. I love you.

And last but not least, to all my other great friends who travel with me on revivals. Thanks for being with me on special trips and for believing in me and trusting me.

$\mathcal{I}$NTRODUCTION

When we are born, we have no idea how our lives will turn out. Growing up, I never knew I would face the things I did. However, it was all in God's plan for my life. In this book, you will read how I was nearly killed time and again and how the devil set a trap for my life while providing me with everything I ever wanted to keep me his slave and to try to destroy my life. I wanted to make it big in the big city with all the bright lights. I had so much money I didn't know what to do with it.

That was my goal – to have money, money, money, and to be in movies and theaters, I thought. I was on my way. However, God had a plan laid out for me that looked very different. It included being saved, preaching His Word and living for Him. The devil thought he had me – but only God did in the end.

This book is my life story. In earlier years, I was on a roller coaster headed straight for hell. But God showed me visions and gave me my family. As I look back over my life, I can and do give God all the glory, honor and praise for saving me, keeping me and giving me His love. If you don't have love, you don't have anything. God's love kept me every time a gun was pointed at my head, every time I was beaten and every time the devil himself tried to kill me. May this book bless you as you read it, and may you know that God is a keeper and He will never leave you nor forsake you. Remember, Jesus loves you, and so do I.

Evangelist Bonnie Baker

Then – Twenty-eight years ago

ONE

In the *Beginning*

My Childhood

I was born in the small town of Vredenburgh, Alabama (population 500), to Jack and Clara Richardson, the seventh of ten children. When I was born, the devil immediately tried to kill me. He attacked me with double pneumonia, and I had to stay in the hospital for two months before I was well enough to go home.

In all I had seven brothers: Jack, Burlee, James, Clarence, Armie, Alexander and Nathaniel; and two sisters: Barbara and Emma, known as Hattie.

As a child, I got into all kinds of trouble. When I was between four and six years old, I would dance for my family, especially my eldest brother, for pennies, nickels and dimes. This is when the seeds were planted – the love of dancing and the love of money.

When I was growing up, our home was the center of attraction. One reason was we had a television. Even though we had an outhouse, we were one of the first families to have a television and a telephone. Also, neighborhood boys would come to our house to play ball on my brothers' baseball diamond.

When we were kids, our family washed clothes in a large black boiling pot. We grew peach trees, pecan trees, corn, beans, okra, sweet potatoes, tomatoes, greens and sugar cane. We ate meat from pigs and chickens that we raised as well as fish that my parents caught. I walked to school every day, thirty minutes each way.

In our small town, everyone knew everyone. Our town had one general store, where we would buy items on credit. It took about twenty minutes to walk to the store. We had to walk there barefoot, and in the summer, the hot blacktop road would burn our feet. We occasionally made shoes from aluminum pop cans, milk cartons, pieces of wood and rubber bands. We would smash the cans with our feet until we molded them to fit.

My dad worked at the sawmill and drove a truck. Meanwhile, my mom cooked for everyone. A potbelly stove provided us with heat. It was my responsibility to make a fire each morning at five o'clock. If I overslept and my mother woke up before I made the fire, it felt as if a fire had been lit on my backside. In fact, one of my brothers and I apparently received the most whippings of the siblings.

At age ten, the devil tried to kill me again. I almost drowned while at the beach in Pensacola, Florida. I was on a field trip with my fourth-grade class, and a little boy I liked told me to go with him into the water. I went in, and he left me standing there. Immediately, the waves rolled in and took me under. I received mouth-to-mouth resuscitation and was revived. But as I grew older, the devil continued to try to take my life. One time was when I was twelve and I was almost beaten to death.

In the Beginning

Despite these tragedies, I was popular in school. In ninth grade, I was chosen both Homecoming Queen and Miss Vredenburgh High. During homecoming festivities, I wore a crown and had two attendants in my court. This was a big deal for me, and a large part of the town was present on the Crowning of the Queens Night. The homecoming parade took place the next morning; we rode in cars and on floats. Also as part of the homecoming festivities, we went to J.F. Shield High School in Beatrice, Alabama, where homecoming queens and their attendants from nearby towns came together to socialize.

The Teen Years

At age fifteen, I gave my life to the Lord and was saved. I was a member of a singing group at church. One night after singing in church, I was in my parents' bedroom, and the power of God hit me. I began to sing the song "Call Him Up" loudly. The power of God rested heavily on me until I saw a light. I followed the light through several doors. I began to yell so loudly that my parents thought I had lost my mind. They became nervous and upset, and I shouted until I passed out.

However, although I was truly saved, I did not have the Holy Ghost; therefore, I had no keeping power. I stayed saved for only about a year and a half, then I turned my back on God in favor of something I loved – dancing.

When I was seventeen, separated from God, I married my first husband just to get out of my parents' house because my dad was so strict. I was married for eight months. My husband beat me badly and would not allow me to go out of the house. I was living in hell. Finally, one of my brothers came and took me back to our parents' home, but I did not want to live with my mother and father anymore.

3

Then AND *Now*

At the time, my sister Barbara lived in Detroit, and she said I could stay with her. Even in Detroit, far away from my troubles, the devil still had a contract out on my life. I became involved with a man and began using different drugs with him. The week after I stopped seeing him, he was found shot to death in his mother's driveway. Had that been an ordinary night, I would have been in the car with him and would have been killed too because every night we would sit in the car and talk. Again, someone was praying for me, and the devil's plan to kill me was aborted.

Then my life again seemed like a roller coaster ride. The next man I started seeing was a pimp. It seemed as if I always picked the wrong men. But this man took me through. I wanted to be someone big.

The Big City

I thought, I am in Detroit, the big city. I was so happy to be there. I would have my boyfriend drive me all over the big city just to look at the beautiful lights and tall buildings, I thought, because where I came from, there were no lights and it was pitch black. In Detroit, I would jump up and down and shout, "Look at the beautiful lights." When it snowed, Barbara and I would sit by the window and watch the snow fall for hours. I would take my boyfriend's Cadillac and do donuts in the snow. Wow, what fun this was! I was in the big city, and I was enjoying it all. Then I thought, I can make it BIG.

TWO

The Street Life

Show Me the Money

The pimp introduced me to the bar life. He began taking me to the bar night after night to see if I would like it. We would sit and drink for hours while he informed me of how much money I could make being a barmaid. He pointed out men groping the barmaids while giving them money. He told me: "You can do the same thing and make lots of money. Will you do it for me? Do you love me?" He looked me in my eyes and said, "Do it for me."

I said, "Okay, I will do it. I will be a barmaid for you." At nineteen years old, I was immature and innocent and didn't know what I was getting into. We left but returned the next day so I could apply for a barmaid position. Shortly after that, I became a barmaid and began making lots of money. Life was getting good, or so I thought. After all, I had never had that kind of money before. I remembered when I was at my parents' home and two or three dollars seemed like a lot of money. But when I began making this kind of money, I jumped for joy to be able to hold a ten, twenty or fifty dollar bill in my hands. I thought I was in heaven and thought I had it going on.

The sad part was I didn't end up keeping a dime of the money. I had to give every penny to my pimp. The Bible states that money is the root of all evil, and I was no exception.

One Horrifying Evening

One night while working as a barmaid, I met a man who said he would give me a lot of money if I would go home with him. Not knowing anything about this kind of life, I said, "Yes, I'll go home with you." I didn't know that would bring me face-to-face with death. We left the bar around 2 A.M. supposedly to go to his house. But I found out he didn't have a house. He took me to his friend's apartment. And when we arrived, there were six more men there.

The man I left the bar with immediately changed. It seemed as if the devil had entered his body. He started calling me out of my name and saying terrible things to me. He said, "I will not give up a dime, and you are going to do everything I say." I was so afraid that I did just that. The men proceeded to tie me up and tape my mouth shut so I couldn't scream. At this point, they pulled out guns to let me see them. Then they told me if I tried anything, they would kill me.

The man began to rape me over and over again. When he finished with me, he told each of the other men to rape me too. One by one, each man raped me over and over again. I went through five hours of torture as all seven men raped me. During this period, I continued slipping in and out of consciousness. It felt as if my insides were torn up. I thought, I don't want to live anymore. They have messed up my body.

At that point, it was approximately 7:30 in the morning and all the men were high. The man who brought me to the apartment said to one of the other men, "Okay, you can kill her now and put her body out in the big dumpster in the alley." Then one man pulled out a gun and pointed it at my head. I could not run, move or get up. I thought I was dead. I began to go back over and examine my life. I thought I would never see my mother or father again. I thought I would never have children. I began to wish I had died from pneumonia when I was an infant.

After being raped continuously for five hours, my body was weak, and I was totally out of it. At the time, I was just nineteen years old and weighed between eighty-eight and ninety pounds.

Another one of the seven men threatened to kill me, and I passed out. When I came to, they were slapping me and calling me out of my name. I got up slowly and tried to walk as they continued to kick me and call me terrible names. Walking was extremely difficult, but I made it outside. The man who said he would kill me put me in his car and drove away.

I had tears in my eyes and rolling down my face. But the man said: "Tell me where you live. I am not going to kill you. I had to do what I did to you inside that apartment, or they would have killed me and called me a punk." He said, "I'm sorry for what they did to you."

I looked at him and didn't know if he was going to kill me or not. I said with a weak voice, "You are going to take me home?"

He said, "Yes, I'm taking you home."

I would have gone immediately to the hospital, but I could not walk well and I was in so much pain.

As we drove, he said, "You know, my mother is saved, and I should be also." I did not say anything because I still didn't know whether he was going to kill me. He continued to talk as we rode along. I lost sight of the location of the apartment and where I had been. All I knew was it seemed far away.

As we got close to my apartment, my heart began to weep and my soul began to get happy. He began to cry and said, "Miss, I am so sorry for what I and my friends did to you." Once we reached the apartment, I could not get out of the car. He came around to my side of the car and helped me get out. I did not say anything. He said, "Don't let her die."

Trying to walk, I constantly fell, got up, fell again and got up again until I reached my apartment door. I looked back to see him still sitting in the car. I remember thinking, He is going to come in and kill me. But at that point, I didn't care anymore. I knew I had to make it to the bed or I would pass out right there and die. I had not eaten for a day and a half, and I was extremely weak.

Later that morning, my pimp came over and said: "What's wrong with you? Get up. We're going to the bar." But I could not move. My legs and thighs were badly swollen, and walking was still extremely painful. I told my pimp what had happened, but he did not believe me. I had cried so much and so hard that I could not cry anymore. I just wanted to go back home to my mother and father. However, my pimp told me he loved me, and that was all I wanted to hear.

Time passed, and I recovered and returned to the bar. I remembered saying that being a barmaid was not for me because there wasn't a lot of money in it and I had to make big money.

Dancing the Night Away

Next my pimp introduced me to go-go dancing. I auditioned to be a dancer and got the job. I began dancing at several clubs. I began drinking, meeting people and making lots of money. I thought I was making money being a barmaid, but I made more money dancing. The other dancers had told me it was easy to make lots of money in this business and, of course, this sounded good to me. I thought I had struck it rich, and I thought I was all that and a bag of chips. I worked from noon until 2 A.M. I danced so much that when I retired for the night, I was still dancing. At that time, dancing was all I knew. However, the bar life took a toll on my life.

It seemed like every man who came into the bar wanted to buy me drinks and wanted me to sit with him. The men also wanted me to do table dances for a hundred dollars or more. Big money was made from table dancing and regular dancing. Even though the bar was raided many times and we would go to jail for indecent exposure, our boss would get us out, and we would be back dancing again until the bar closed. I became so popular that men would come in and ask for me. This made the bar manager happy because they enjoyed seeing girls mingling with the men and having men buy them drinks.

My income from dancing increased several times, and I was to tell no one about it. I gave all the money I made to my pimp. I continued to go-go dance, and I made big money. I became very famous and made so much money that I was just not ready to get out yet. I had my own little act that would get me into the movies and on stage in theaters. I was on my way to making it huge.

Then one night at about 1:45 A.M., just before the bar closed at 2 A.M., some people held up the bar. After the grand finale, while we girls were in the dressing room, still in our costumes, we heard someone say, "You know what time it is?" We thought someone was playing a joke. Then three men with guns knocked down our door and said:

"You know what time it is? Give up your money and get down on the floor."

Then they looked at me and said, "You come with us." Out of all the girls in the room, they picked me to come with them. They said to me, "Take this hat, go around to everyone on the floor, and get their money and their wallets. One man covered the locked door; one man stood in the middle of the floor; one man followed me around with a gun, calling me all sorts of names. He kept saying, "Hurry up before I blow your brains out." At one point, he placed the gun at my head and began pulling the trigger. Thank God the gun did not fire.

After we got all the money and wallets from everyone in the bar, they told me to lie down on the floor and keep my head down. Then they went out the back door of the bar. They said if I looked up they would blow my head off. I got on the floor and cried. I heard the back door close, and I said, "They're gone." My boss was seriously injured from being pistol-whipped. Blood was running down his face. A few of the customers also were hurt. Often in hostage situations, the hostage is killed. But again, someone was praying for me, and I was not injured.

When the police arrived, they asked who had seen the men. Then they called me. I didn't want any part of it, so I said I did not remember how the men looked. I was so afraid I tried not to look at the police. However, I knew it was some men who had been in the bar on numerous occasions. After that ordeal, I began to live in hotels. They became my home with my pimp. I took time off from work because I had enough money to do that.

When I became a go-go dancer, my pimp would beat me until I became afraid to leave him. He said he would kill me if I did. And I had to give him every penny I earned from dancing.

The Street Life

Rising Popularity

My popularity as a dancer was soaring. During this time, many of my girlfriends were reported missing and many were found dead, which made me afraid. However, I continued dancing and became even more famous in the dance world. I no longer danced in the Detroit area. Instead I traveled to all parts of Canada.

I had two stage names: Little Chocolate Chip and Sweet Brown Sugar. As they introduced me and my acts, the announcers would say, "Here comes Chocolate Chip, the one and only, the famous cigarette girl." I was big.

THREE

A LIVING HELL

The Only Girl for Him

My pimp had decided to let all his other girls go. I was the only one he kept. I met his family and became close with them. It was his mother who introduced me to gambling and playing cards. My pimp became jealous. One night his mother and I decided we were going out to play cards. He didn't believe this, and as a result, we got into a bad fight. He broke both my jaws. At that time, my brother had just gotten out of the Air Force and was living with us. When he saw blood all over me and realized I was unable to speak (my mouth was twisted from one side to the other), he was furious. My brother wanted to kill my pimp.

Meanwhile, other people in the apartment building had heard our fight and had come over to my apartment. They called the police. Although I was unable to speak, I motioned with my body, flinging my arms, making grunting sounds and beating my chest in an effort to try to let my brother know it was my fault, not my pimp's. I begged and pleaded with my brother not to kill him. I tried to communicate to my brother that we had had a fight because I was planning to go out and he did not want me to go. I kept trying to tell my brother that it was all my fault.

A few minutes later, the police arrived and took my pimp to jail. An ambulance also arrived and took me to Henry Ford Hospital. I was hospitalized for six weeks. The surgeon had to put my entire mouth back into place. Besides two broken jaws, I also sustained a concussion. Four screws were placed in my left jaw to hold it in place. As a result of the screws in my jaw, to this day, I have no feeling in my jaw. I can tell when it's going to rain because the screws begin to itch.

I had said I did not want to see my pimp again. But after being released from jail, he came to the hospital to see me. I told him I didn't want to see him anymore, and he left the hospital so upset that he stood on the cement and yelled, "Bonnie, Bonnie!" He was so loud, the hospital staff had him arrested for disturbing the other patients.

While I remained in the hospital, the only way I could eat or drink was through a straw. This lasted for eight weeks. Needless to say, it was decided that I be placed on a liquid diet.

Once released from the hospital, I saw my pimp again. And once again, he told me he loved me. He said he was sorry and asked me to marry him. Thinking I was so in love with him, I said, "Yes, I will marry you." We were soon married. My family didn't want this to happen, but at the time, I did not care. I thought I was in love. Plus, we had been through a lot together.

Although my brother was still upset with me about my pimp, I just wanted to be with him. My brother said he should have shot my pimp and been sent to jail. I would have married him regardless. My whole family was hurt because I married the man who introduced me to this lifestyle, the man who constantly beat me.

You see, the devil still had a contract out on my life. However, although he had controlled my life, God had mapped out my life. My grandmother, mother and sister had gotten saved and had given their lives to the Lord. They began to pray for me all the time.

The Abuse Continues

After I married my pimp, I brought him to meet my family. They did not like him. After we were married, he did stop beating me –for a while. But then he started again, and I went through one beating after another. Eventually, I got tired of the beatings and tried to kill him. He also tried to kill me. I was living in hell and did not know how to get out. The devil made it look so good, but all the time he was trying to take me straight to hell with him.

Many times I thought I was going to die. It was like I was in a box and could not get out. This husband tried to kill me on many, many occasions. One time he choked me so hard that I saw stars, foam ran down both sides of my mouth, and my eyes rolled back into my head. It was at that point that I thought it was over. I thought, This is it. I began holding my breath to make him think he had choked me to death. He then got up and said: "I did not mean to kill you. Wake up, Bonnie. Wake up!" I continued to hold my breath until the bitter end. I knew if he thought I was still alive and breathing, he would have finished me off. When he walked away and went into the living room, I got up, ran to the back door, opened it and ran down the street naked yelling, "Help! Help! Help!"

Then I realized I had to leave this man or I would die. The next time I saw him I told him I was leaving him. He laughed and said: "Right! I will kill you. Don't you know this? If you leave me, I will find you and kill you."

I had stayed married to him, my second husband, longer than I did to my first husband, but I kept my promise. I left him.

Next I met another man involved with drugs. I lived with him for months in a hotel. But I found out I had gotten out of one bad situation and into a worse one. This man was well-known, and people had been looking for him. He had been shot before. My life again became a roller coaster with a merry-go-round effect. I was constantly getting involved with the wrong people.

This man had a friend who had a big hit (drugs that he did not pay for). There was a contract out on him. One night we were at a restaurant, and as we were getting ready to leave, people were waiting outside to kill him. We rode down Davidson Avenue while the people in the car behind us shot at us as in the movies. The friend's girlfriend and I were on the floor; the men had told us to stay down. The people in the other car continued to shoot at us. We traveled south on the Lodge Freeway, then east on Interstate 94, and we lost them. To keep from being found, we went to a filthy hotel and hid out for a week.

Then I began to think about my future. When I left my second husband, I had decided I would get a real job, either in the plants or somewhere else. But the devil had set up and devised a plan for me.

FOUR

ALL THE WRONG RELATIONSHIPS

The Preacher

At this time in my life, I wanted to get right with God. I began going to church to try to get my life together. I met a preacher who knew I was a go-go dancer but started to like me. I had heard that he could give out good numbers to play in the lottery, and if you played the numbers he gave out, you would hit. The girls who took me to his church had hit many times before and had won big money. One girl said, "I know he'll like you because you are small and petite just like he likes them. You will get lots of numbers."

The first Sunday I went to church, I really went to get something from God. But something wasn't right with the preacher. All during the service, he watched me. As he got up to preach, he began to say, "My shoes are hot. My shoes are hot. My shoes are hot." My friend said: "Girl, get on shoes and play that in the lottery. Stay on it for three days, and you will hit because this man is good."

"Okay," I said. "I will play shoes for three days." I did so, and I hit on the second day. Before the service was over, he called for an offering, and I gave fifty dollars. The preacher thought this was a large offering for a small church. He had me stand and wanted to see me after the service.

I went to his office, and he said: "You are so pretty. How long have you been a go-go dancer?"

I responded, "About nine years so far."

He asked me if I would dance for him. Then he said, "I can help you make a lot of money."

"How is that?" I asked.

He said: "The Lord has given me to call out numbers, and you can hit. Play shoes for three days. This is my number; call me after you hit." I then made him one of my sugar daddies to get money. This preacher was leading all the members astray. I knew he was not right, but as long as I was making money, I didn't care. I continued going to that church for five or six months and kept seeing the preacher. He had a very nice wife.

One Sunday he said: "I want to see you. Can you meet me at the hotel?" I said I would. I got to the hotel, and he told me to be at church Sunday because he was giving out his last number. He said God told him if he did not stop giving out numbers and doing people wrong, He was going to lay him flat on his back and he would not be able to move. I became afraid.

However, I did go to church that Sunday, and I could tell the preacher was sick. He looked weak. In his message, he called out, "Fire, fire, fire, fire, fire," but he did not say how long to play it. I got on it and began playing it heavy, putting big money on it. I played this number for three days, then I stopped. On the fourth day, the number hit.

I went to the preacher and asked, "Why didn't you say the number was hitting on the fourth day?"

He said, "You know I'm very sick."

Again I asked, "Why didn't you say the number would hit on the fourth day?"

"Remember, I said it five times. You should have stayed on it for five days."

After that, he became so sick, almost to the point of death, and he had to be hospitalized. He said the Lord spoke to him and instructed him to inform the church of his wrongdoings and to ask for forgiveness from the church and from his wife. He said the Lord also told him he could not be a pastor any longer or he would die and go to hell. This would be a result of leading God's people astray.

After that, I broke ties with the preacher and moved on to the next man. I developed a serious drinking problem. I would consume so much alcohol that I wouldn't remember how I made it home. The bar life had taken a toll on me. I was battling with the devil, and he almost won. I became so depressed that I thought about killing myself. I wanted to leave this earth because I was tired of the life I was living. Although I had been involved in everything, had done everything and had everything, even money, I was lonely, hurt and in need of something I was not getting.

I needed God. My sister, mother and grandmother had been praying for my salvation. I knew the way, but I didn't want to give up all the money the devil had me making. However, I realized God was not blessing me.

The Police Officer

The next man I became involved with was a police officer. He was a sergeant. We started seeing each other. I had gotten to know all of his friends, and his friends knew me.

Then AND *Now*

My dancing friend and I often performed private parties for some of the officers. But he had a wife and a baby. I destroyed his marriage and his home because I wanted him for myself. And he became so possessive of me that he didn't want me seeing anyone else, including my seven other sugar daddies who kept me supplied with large sums of money.

Before his wife found out about me and left him, I almost killed him. I told him I was going to start seeing someone else, someone who could spend the night with me, something he couldn't do being married. One night when he started to leave, I got my gun and fired at him. I would have shot him had my hand not gone up in the air while firing the gun. I shot and shot and shot until I emptied the barrel and all the bullets were used. He jumped in the police car and left. Later he called me and said, "You shot at me!" I said, "I know. Next time I won't miss."

That was more than twenty-three years ago, and had I killed the officer, I still would not be up for parole. I felt really bad for him when his wife left because I knew it was because of me.

At that time in my life, all of my dancing friends were taking drugs or drinking heavily. The bar life was taking a toll on all of us. I carried a gun I had gotten from my daddy everywhere I went. I was walking a death row experience while thinking I was bad. After coming close to dying so many times, it didn't matter to me whether I lived or died. The devil had my life all planned out. But someone was praying for me, and God had His hands on my life. One positive note was I loved my family – my mother, father, sisters and brothers – and it was nothing for me to send my parents large sums of money.

All the Wrong Relationships

Sugar Daddies

After my relationship with the police officer ended, I became involved with several sugar daddies because of the money I could get from them. All together, I had seven sugar daddies. One of them begged me to give up dancing. He said he would marry me and take care of me. However, he was about twenty-six years older than I was, and I didn't want to be married anymore at that time. This sugar daddy constantly talked to the dead. His wife of 45 years had died. He told her about me, and she said I was his wife. He was so heavy into witchcraft that he could and would make the lights in my house turn on and off. He would tell me things that would happen.

Again, I thank God for my sister. She saw it in the spirit, and she and her twin sister in the Gospel prayed me out of that situation. He had refused to let me go because he said his dead wife told him not to let me go. She supposedly said, "You have given her over thirty-five thousand dollars. She is your wife."

I believe this sugar daddy would have killed me had God not been on my side. He was extremely possessive of me. He documented everything we did, including every time he saw me and all the money he gave me. It was nothing for him to tell me how much money he had given me. During all this, the devil yet had me on his hit list. And I was living all I knew for the devil because most of the time, I didn't want to be saved.

Later I decided to move to California, where I began auditioning for movies. I was determined to make it big. Little did I realize that my lifestyle was in the completion phase, and God was about to save me. I thought I was getting things in place, and I was going to make my own shows and movies. I finally had arrived. I was where I wanted to be.

21

Then AND *Now*

My sugar daddy had wanted nothing from me but marriage. But despite all the money he gave me, I couldn't marry him. I believe he knew something was happening that was causing me to change. I began to act differently. Even my last dance was different. I could not get things together. It was at that point that I felt my life changing. However, the devil still had a stronghold on me. I still did not want to be saved because I was making too much money and I did not want to give all of that up.

FIVE

INTERCESSORY PRAYER

My Sister

My sister in North Carolina never wanted any of my "dirty" money. She always felt I would get killed by one of my sugar daddies because of all the money they gave me. She began to pray hard for me. I remember her calling me frequently and telling me what the Lord showed her about me in dreams. She saw me drowned, beat to death, killed in a car accident and so on. I had the nerve to tell her: "Thank you, sister. I'm going to play that in the lottery, and when I hit, I will send you some money."

She would say: "I've got to go. I'm praying for you."

On one occasion, one of my sugar daddies took me to London, and my sister prayed that I would not enjoy the trip. Her prayers worked. When we arrived in London, my sugar daddy wanted me to go with him to see the city. I didn't want to go. Instead, I wanted him to go and get me two packs of cigarettes. I stayed in the hotel for three days. Then

I called my mother to tell her what my sister had said. I wondered why she didn't want me to enjoy myself. I asked my mother to pray that I would have a good time while I was in London, and I told her I didn't want this man to hurt me.

She said, "Okay." On the fourth day, I went out but did not enjoy myself. My sister was and is a praying woman of God. Every word she has given me has come to pass, and this was no exception. While I was in my sin, she told the devil he would not have me. I was already in hell, and she saw this in the spirit. While in the spirit, she snatched me out of the devil's hell. She prayed and fasted, along with her twin sister in the Lord. One day she called, and I said: "Okay, what is it this time? Did I die yet"? I grieved her spirit so many times because of what I would say, the way I would live and the things I would do. However, she looked beyond all of that and never stopped praying for me.

Prayer changes things! The prayer of a righteous man or woman avails much.

My sweet sister intervened again one Friday at about 11 P.M. She called and said, "Bonnie, I'm going to tell you the vision God just showed me." As usual, I said, "Okay, let's hear it." Her voice was serious as she said, "God said don't go back to Canada anymore. The family had to come and identify you. You had a tag on your big toe." She said, "Don't go back up there. I have given you everything God has given me. This time, this is it."

This time her words scared me. I didn't tell her I had been in Canada. Even in my sin, I realized God gave my sister this. In the past when my sister would call and give me a word from the Lord, I never felt like this. Nevertheless, I played it off and didn't let her know how it affected me. I told her I would play that in the lottery. She said, "I love you, and I will talk to you later."

I said, "Okay" and hung up the phone. I immediately began to cry. I couldn't shake what my sister had said to me. I was so troubled that I cried until I fell asleep that night. I almost got sick from crying so much. I felt that this time I would die. I kept hearing my sister say my family came to identify my body and I had a tag on my big toe. I could picture this, and it was scary.

The next morning, despite my sister's warning, my girlfriend and I were on our way to Niagara Falls, Canada, to make big money. The weather was awful, and the roads were bad. The farther we traveled from Detroit, the more it snowed. In my brand new 1980 Lincoln, I moved into the fast lane and remained there for some time. All of a sudden, I began to slide from one lane to another. I slid a long distance off the expressway and almost ended up in a river. As the car began to go down, I saw hell. It was black, extremely black. I said, "If I'm going to die this morning, I am not going by myself." I grabbed my girlfriend by the collar and said, "You are going to die with me." We both screamed.

When the car landed, I opened my eyes and said, "I'm still here!" As we looked up toward the expressway, we heard people calling us. They wondered if we were all right. The police came and called the tow truck to pull us out. Once we got out, we went to the gas station across the street and stayed there awhile. While sitting there, again I heard my sister say my family came to identify my body and I had a tag on my big toe. This was ringing in my spirit.

At that point, we should have gone back home. But despite my sister's words and the roads becoming more treacherous, we continued on because we were thinking of all the money we could make in Canada. Later I lost control of my car, and we ended up hitting a light pole. The car almost turned over. Again I heard my sister's words. Yet after we pulled ourselves together, we continued on our way. Music was playing on the radio, and I turned the volume up to try to drown out my sister's voice in my head. I began to think that day would be the day I would die. I had tasted death many times before, but this time was different. I turned the radio off and told my friend what my sister had said to me during our last phone conversation. Fear gripped my friend too.

In spite of all the warnings, we continued on to Canada to make money. However, as we approached the hotel, we almost had a head-on collision with another car. Thankfully, both cars stopped in time to avoid the collision. My sister's words came to haunt me again. I told my friend I needed a drink. I told her as soon as we arrived at the hotel, I would get so drunk that I would no longer hear my sister's words, and that's exactly what I did. I was so drunk I don't know how I made it to my room. The next morning, I was sick from drinking so much.

Once my girlfriend and I returned from Canada, I called my sister. She was surprised to hear from me. I began to talk to her, but I didn't tell her what had happened. I wanted to see if she knew. She told me that she lay before the Lord the whole week for me. She was unable to eat until the Lord released her spirit concerning me. At that point, I realized prayer was the only reason I made it home safely. The entire time I was in Canada, my mother, my sister and my sister's twin sister in the Gospel had prayed for me. And because of their prayers, the devil had to release me and let me go.

While luring me to hell with him, the devil gave me everything I thought I wanted. He will make things appear good. However, he won't show you that his goal is to take you to hell. I was totally sold out to the devil. I was a walking time bomb going straight to hell. I thank God I had someone praying for me and keeping me up before God while in my sin. I was running and crying, and I didn't know why. I had it all, and yet I was lost, unhappy, lonely and depressed, realizing all the times the devil had tried unsuccessfully to kill me. My mind went back to the eighth floor of the hotel in Canada, where the devil continued to tell me to jump, jump, jump! I became so confused I didn't know what to do. Then from nowhere, I began to inwardly pray, "Help me, Lord. Help me." Had I jumped, I would not be here today to tell my story.

Again I offered to send my sister some money. And again she said she did not want it. Then she said, "I'll be praying for you." She wouldn't take anything from me, which made her get on my nerves. But all she wanted was for me to be saved and to live for the Lord. Little did she know her wishes soon would come true. That was in 1981, and my time in the devil's world was quickly coming to an end. I was about to be saved.

Getting Saved

The devil knew his time was almost up. He didn't want me to give my heart to the Lord, and he was fighting it. He told me just to kill myself right there in that hotel, and I considered doing just that. I was about to jump out the hotel window when my girlfriend knocked at the door and said, "Bonnie, open the door. I have to tell you how much money I made. We have a show at 2 P.M."

I listened to her while also listening to the devil. I thought about what my sister had said – how she would always say she was praying for me and that the devil would not have me! The devil intensified his talking to me. He said: "You've had it all. What more is there for you to get? Jump! Just jump!" But my friend insisted I open the door. I thought I was through and it was over. I was at the window with tears in my eyes, ready to jump. My heart was beating fast. I began to say, "Help me, Lord!" I had not said that since I was saved at age fifteen. I was at my wits end and I said, "Lord, please help me!" At that very moment my friend said, "If you don't open this door, I will go and get the manager."

I turned and went to the door and opened it. She said, "What is wrong with you, girl? Have you lost your mind? Come and have a drink with me." She told me about all the money she had made the night before, and I didn't say a word. I had four or five drinks and told my friend that I was going to kill myself. She hugged me, cried and pleaded with me not to think that way again. She said, "We are going to make big, big money."

However, at that point, I didn't care if I made any money. All I wanted was to go be with my mother, father and family. I didn't care about the money anymore. A change had taken place in my life. Little did I know that this would be my last dance.

Then my mind went back to the times I was raped repeatedly, and I wanted to get revenge against all those men. Because of the hurt and pain I had experienced, I didn't care about destroying homes or taking men's money. I didn't care about anything. I wanted to use men like I had been used that night I was raped. I was bitter. I was unable to forgive my second husband, the pimp, for breaking my jaws, breaking my arms, burning my shoulder, giving me black eyes and the list goes on. Every time I spoke to my second husband, he would ask me to forgive him. I would remind him that because of him, I had to be cut under my jaw, and the scar would forever be there. I would ask why he did it, and he would say because he was drinking and doing drugs, and then say that he was eternally sorry. He would say he never should have hurt me, and I said he was right.

Years passed, and I did not hear from him. However, shortly before he died from cancer, he had his aunt call me and ask me to talk to him. I did, and again he asked me to forgive him for the way he had treated me. He said he was dying from cancer and he felt this was happening to him because of his behavior toward me. In the past, I had always found myself getting angry with him when he asked for forgiveness. And until this time, I was unaware that I still held bitterness toward him in my heart. But after praying, I finally was able to tell him I forgave him. I asked him if he had made things right with God, and he said he thought God had forgiven him. I attended his funeral and while there, I felt a weight had been lifted off me. I felt light and free.

After the second man I had a relationship with who was involved with drugs died, I attended his funeral and found the same thing happened – a weight was lifted from me, and I felt free.

I began to realize that from the second day I was born, the devil desired to take me out. All my life he had set traps to destroy me, kill me and take me to hell with him. How I thank God that He had other plans for my life, plans I knew nothing about – eternal life in heaven.

In the past, I would sit and cry night after night, wondering why all these things had happened to me. I wondered why I couldn't be happy, why all my friends were drug addicts or alcoholics, why the devil constantly surrounded me with the wrong crowd. Had it not been for the Lord being on my side, I would have been dead and buried in my grave, living in hell, only to be tormented forever.

I remember one time I was with a friend for a week. Days later, her body was found behind a bar, her neck cut. Many of my dancer friends had ended up missing or dead. I really became frightened by this, and before God called me in, the devil allowed me to make so much money that I wasn't ready to give up this lifestyle. One night I had all my money lying on the bed. I was literally scared because I had never seen that much money before. Still the devil started talking to me, saying: "This is nothing. You can have it all!" I looked at the money and cried. The devil showed me what I had, and he showed me how much more I could have. In spite of this, I knew God was calling me unto salvation, and everything I did after that didn't feel right.

In the early eighties, I began to hate what I was doing. I wasn't happy living that life anymore. I did not know that God would save me in 1982. But the devil didn't give up. Again he tried to destroy me by almost causing a terrible accident that surely would have taken my life. Because I wore an expensive gold chain, the devil set me up to be robbed. My friend whom I hung out with at that time began to turn on me and took things from me. At the same time, I began gambling heavy. I lost all my money throwing dice and playing cards. I knew it was time to give it all up. However, things became worse, as the first thing I thought about was how to get more money. I reverted back to my old lifestyle, even more so, and again I made big, big, big, big money!

In 1982, I went back to Canada. As they introduced me, they said: "Everyone, you remember Little Chocolate Chip. She's back performing her cigarette girl act." I was back for the last time. That ended up being the last dance I performed for the devil.

By then, Christmas was approaching. That Christmas, all of us – my six brothers, my two sisters and me – went to my parents' home for the holiday. When I saw my sister from North Carolina, I said hi. As she hugged me, I heard her say: "Save her this year. God, save her now." I thought, I'm tired of her now. In Detroit, I received phone call after phone call from her telling me I was going to die. It's now Christmas, and we're at our parents' home. I don't want to hear this. However, I did fear her a little because you could see the power and glory of God in her.

The next morning, we were all sitting around talking when I began to sing loudly: "This little light of mine, I've got to let it shine. Let it shine, let it shine, let it shine." My sister looked at me and said out loud, "Lord, let it become real in her now." I laughed and continued to sing. I wanted to make her happy so she would stop with all the praying and seeing things.

We all had a good time at our parents' home. While there, my sister was trying to get us to come through Greenville, North Carolina, to see them on our way home. I didn't know this was a setup. But she and her twin sister in the Gospel had it all planned out: If I went to North Carolina, they would take me to church. Therefore, she told me what day to leave to head back, and what day to come to North Carolina.

My brother had just gotten a new van, and that Christmas, my sugar daddy and I rode with my brother, his wife and their children. So I told my sister that if I could get our brother to bring us to North Carolina on our way back to Detroit, we would come. And I said I would go to church so she would stop bugging me about the dreams and visions she had had about me. My brother said he would bring us to North Carolina if I paid for the gas. This, of course, was no problem.

So we left our parents' home early Tuesday morning and started on our way to North Carolina. This should have placed us in North Carolina at around four o'clock in the afternoon. However, we ran a little late and didn't arrive in North Carolina until about 7:30 P.M.

As soon as we arrived at one brother's home, also in Greenville, I called to let my sister know we were there. I asked if it was too late to go to church and she said, "No, we are waiting for you." I asked who "we" was, and she said her twin sister in the Gospel and her. I told her to let me change clothes, then my sugar daddy and I would be over.

My brother and sister lived just about three minutes apart. It was approximately 8 P.M. when we arrived at my sister's home. She introduced me to her sister in the Gospel, who today is our adopted sister because our mother spiritually adopted her. She is also our daughter's Godmother.

That night, I, my sugar daddy, my sister and her sister in the Gospel got in the car and started on our way. Along the way, I heard them praying. I was thinking that after this, I didn't want her to call me anymore about this salvation stuff. I was going to church with her so she would leave me alone. Then I heard them say: "Save her, Lord, this night. Devil, we claim her soul this night." But the devil didn't surrender yet, and I thought, They can pray all they want. That is not going to happen.

We finally arrived at church, my sister tried to sit us in the front of the church. I said we didn't want to sit that far up, so they sat farther back with us. About fifteen minutes into the church service, the pastor asked if anyone wanted to be saved. I sat there for a minute, and they were praying. I thought that if I went to the front to be saved, she would leave me alone. So I got up and proceeded to the front of the church. My sugar daddy tried to stop me, but they told him I would be fine.

The pastor called for me, took me through the sinners' prayer and laid hands on me. I fell out under the power of God. I tried to get up, but I couldn't. I could hear the people praising the Lord. I heard my sister tell the people not to touch me and that I would be all right. After I stayed out under the power of God for a while, my sugar daddy came to get me.

On that night in 1982, God saved my life, and my life completely changed after that. After that, my sugar daddy was angry with my sisters. He said that while I was slain by the power of God, my sisters put something on me that changed me. I began seeking the Lord. On January 13, 1983, the Lord filled me with the precious Holy Ghost. That happened between 2 and 3 P.M., and from that point on, I have stayed saved and have lived for Him. I see now that their prayers worked.

After I was saved, I continued to see one of my sugar daddies (the one who was in North Carolina with me when I received salvation). He began attending church with me. We looked funny together, as he was twenty-six years older than me and had white hair. We went together to see Apostle Miles because my sugar daddy led me to believe he wanted to be saved. During our counseling session with Apostle Miles, he asked my sugar daddy if he believed in God. He looked Apostle Miles in his eyes and said, "No, I don't believe there is a God. If there was, he would not have allowed my wife of forty-five years to die." Pastor Miles continued to talk with us for a while. Afterward, he called me and told me I had to let him go. Pastor Miles saw the spirit of witchcraft in him.

I obeyed my pastor and told my sugar daddy I could no longer see him. However, for a long time, he continued to come to church to see me. He would watch our church telecast just to see me and find out when the choir concerts would take place so he could attend. Three years after I was married, he continued to try to see me until he saw I was truly saved and saw the change that occurred in my life. I told him I loved the Lord and I wanted to be saved. He told me I could have all his money. But I didn't want that anymore. My mind was made up not to go back into the life I had left. I had found a new love, and His name was JESUS. I was living for Him now.

Now

SIX

THE *Beginning* OF MY *New Life*

After I Got Saved

In 1982, after I got saved, the Lord filled me with the Holy Ghost. One night I awoke, sat up in bed and began to pray. I looked at my window, and a cross appeared before me in it. I was so afraid. But God said to me, "This is I, Jesus!"

Later on, my sister told me about International Gospel Center, where the late Apostle Charles O. Miles had been the pastor. There was a wonderful fellowship between her church and IGC. Then I found my way to IGC. As I was getting out of my car, my neighbors who lived across the street from me were walking toward the church. I said: "Hi. Do you attend this church?" The husband said, "Yes." I asked if his wife was there, and she was. She sold Avon at one time and would always place Avon brochures at my door. But before my salvation, I did not have time for her or her Avon. I told my neighbor I was now saved, and I wanted to meet his wife.

Then AND *Now*

After we met, we became friends, and we are best friends to this day. My neighbors had been attending IGC for some time, and I would be with them. My sister knew an evangelist, a great woman of God at IGC, and instructed me to get with her and stay with her so she could nourish me in my walk with God. I met her, and she indeed was a great woman of God. She was also a prophetess, a counselor and a teacher. However, she traveled a lot, ministering the Word of God. Since she often was gone, she introduced me to the number one church mother, Mildred Poole. Mother Poole and I became close friends too and developed a mother/daughter relationship. I grew in the Lord as a result of being with Mother Poole. I was living proof of Psalm 92:12, which states: *The righteous shall flourish like the palm tree: he shall grow like a cedar in Lebanon.*

One of my favorite Scriptures that hit home with me is: *For what is a man profited, if he shall gain the whole world, and lose his own soul? or what shall a man give in exchange for his soul?* (Matthew 16:26). I was accustomed to making large sums of money. However, I made it by doing things contrary to the will of God. So when I got saved, I gave it all up. I asked God to save me and to save me real good. I did not want to be one who was in and out of the church. I desired to be completely saved from my head to my toes. When my friends at the bar found out I was saved, they told everyone I would be back within two weeks, after my money ran out. It's been twenty-one years now, and I'm still saved and living for the Lord!

After getting saved, I had to get a job. My first job was at Arby's, and I only worked three hours a day and made thirty dollars a week. After a while, I was promoted to six hours a day and made sixty-eight dollars a week. This was pocket change compared to what I was used to making in the bar, and it was really hurting me. While dancing in the bar, I made one hundred dollars an hour, eight hundred to one thousand dollars a day, four thousand to five thousand dollars a week, sixteen thousand to twenty thousand dollars a month, not to mention my sugar daddies' money and any money I would make from gambling and playing the lottery.

People the Lord Gave Me

Two months after being at IGC, I met my third husband, Mr. Baker. By this time, all of my money was gone, and Mr. Baker and I were now engaged. Six months later, we were married and are still married today, twenty years later. Mother Poole and a close friend coordinated my wedding. God blessed me to meet Gloria, a sweet sister at the church who lived near me. We both were from Alabama. She prayed for me and encouraged me. She gave me clothes to wear because after I got saved, I just had one green dress to wear.

She often told me: "God loves you, and it doesn't matter what you got saved from. I don't look at that, and God doesn't either. Stay saved and continue living for the Lord." She did not look down on me or where I had been. She introduced me to her husband, her two sons and her daughter. I loved her and her family. She was the close friend who helped Mother Poole coordinate my wedding. She was always there for me. She never left me, and to this day, we remain close friends. She is a true woman of God. I would tell her personal things, and never once did I worry about her repeating them to others. Thanks, Gloria, for being there for me, for walking and praying me through until God established me.

Gloria, Marlene and Matthew were like Mother Poole. They took me in and loved me in spite of my past. Thanks, Marlene and Matthew, for also being true friends who were there for me. Thanks for crying with me, laughing with me, praying with me and remaining friends unto this day.

One night in a prayer meeting, Mother Poole asked the members of IGC to bring food to help with my wedding reception. The members did just that, and my reception was very nice – the way the Lord would have it. Mother Poole watched out for me both naturally and spiritually. At that time, I was living alone in the house I had lived in before I got saved. When Mr. Baker came over and stayed past his curfew, the phone would ring, and it would be Mother Poole checking on us. She would ask if he was still there, and if I said he was, she would tell me to tell him it was time for him to leave. I wanted him to stay, but Mother Poole would remain on the phone until he left. She continued to look out for me, even after I married Mr. Baker.

This man is the love of my life, the one God had for me. As I reflect on my life, I thank God for Mother Poole because she kept me in line. Also because of her, I began praying, fasting and seeking the Lord like never before. Mother Poole was a praying mother, and I had to be prayed up to be around her. She loved my husband and me like we were her natural children.

After I started attending the church, when all my money was gone, my neighbors and Mother Poole even helped me pay some of my bills. My neighbors became my very best friends. Mother Poole told me, "Baby, the Lord is going to bless you." She knew the Lord had saved me, and she knew what He was doing for me. She constantly kept me in prayer, and things worked out for me.

At the time when I was really going through, I called Hattie, my sister in North Carolina, and told her this wasn't working for me. She and her husband began sending me money to help in any way they could. Hattie wanted me to stay saved. And I wanted to stay saved because I had found an inner peace and an inner love for which I had been searching. I found this peace and love in Jesus.

But with my money gone, bills became delinquent and things weren't easy. Being married with no money was no fun. My husband and I lived in the same house that all of my sugar daddies, men and everyone in my past had been to. Days after I was married, the police officer from my past came to my house and rang the doorbell. I opened the door, and there he was, looking good. He said, "Hi. How are you?" I said, "Fine." He asked if I was going to invite him in. I said, "No, I'm now married." He said, "Yes, and so was I when you broke up my home." The Bible says in Exodus 20:14: *"Thou shalt not commit adultery."* I told him I had been wrong and I had been in sin. I told him he had to leave, and I told him I was now saved, married and not in that lifestyle anymore.

He said, "Right, I am saved too." He acted as though he didn't believe me. I told him I was sorry for all the pain I had caused him and he had to leave. He said, "I will leave now, but I will be back." Thank God, he never returned.

During this time, I also was behind with my house note and was headed toward foreclosure. Everything seemed out of control. About two weeks later, we were told we had to move. However, God allowed us to stay there for two more years. We had received this word from the Lord. For those two years, we did not pay a penny. God was still looking out for us. We were told we had to pay two thousand dollars to bring the bill current, but we didn't have the money to do that.

I knew I could have made a phone call and had the money we needed to keep our house. However, I didn't make the call because I didn't know how I could explain to my saved husband how I got the money. I had to believe God, as my husband did. We lost that house, and we were set out on the street. All our neighbors saw our things out on the curb. Before my salvation, two thousand dollars would have been easy for me to come up with. And I did not understand why God had allowed me to get saved and then lose all that I had.

But God had other plans for our lives. I later found out that I was not in the blessings of the Lord at that time. Proverbs 10:22 states: *The blessing of the Lord, it maketh rich, and he addeth no sorrow with it.* I finally realized I had to lose all that I had while in the devil's world in order to gain the full blessings of the Lord.

As I continued praying, I would always hear God tell me to give up everything. My answer would always be, "Yes, Lord." And I did. My husband took me to sell all my pretty costumes. With the money we got from selling my diamond "B" necklace, we bought my wedding rings. For one hundred dollars, Dean also sold my 1980 Lincoln Continental. I gathered up my record collection and broke them. Then I gathered all my pictures and cut them up. I didn't want anything that would remind me of my past or where God had brought me from because I was so ashamed.

Recently, God gave me a message titled "Don't Be Ashamed of Your Past; After All, It's Only You!" We know that in Christ, we are new creatures because 2 Corinthians 5:17 states: *"Therefore if any man be in Christ, he is a new creature: old things are passed away; behold, all things are become new."* I was looking for the new.

After being set out on the street, we called Ron and Doris, my brother-in-law and sister-in-law, and asked if we could move in with them. We lived with them for several months. Afterward, we moved into a roach-infested apartment in Inkster, Michigan. The roaches were so bad that when I would open my purse at work, roaches would run out. We really went through. I told the devil at that time: "Devil, if I did not go back on God after losing my house, you can forget it now. For God I live and for God I will die.

I lived for you, devil, and I obeyed you. I have a new boss now Who died for me, and his name is Jesus."

This is reaffirmed in 1 Corinthians 6:19, 20: *"What? know ye not that your body is the temple of the Holy Ghost which is in you, which ye have of God, and ye are not your own? For ye are bought with a price: therefore glorify God in your body, and in your spirit, which are God's."* Glory to God, I am no longer my own. I am bought! Hallelujah! I told the devil: "I will obey Jesus and him only. Get thee hence behind me."

We lived in that apartment for eight months before one of our friends told us about a house for rent. The house was too small for our friend and his family. At that time, we had no children, so the house was the right size for us. We went to look at it, and we told the owner we wanted it. Then we moved from the apartment into the house on Hartwell in Detroit, where we lived for fourteen years.

Meanwhile, Mother Poole was still telling me, "Baby, the Lord will give you back everything you've lost." I would say, "When, Mother Poole, when?" I found my answer in Scripture. Matthew 6:33 says: *"But seek ye first the kingdom of God, and his righteousness; and all these things shall be added unto you."* And Matthew 7:7 states: *"Ask, and it shall be given you; seek, and ye shall find; knock, and it shall be opened unto you."*

Therefore, at that time, we began seeking the Lord like never before. God began speaking to me. He told me He was calling me into the ministry to preach. I became fearful. I began to tell God I couldn't preach because I didn't know what to say. Then the Lord helped me to remember how in my past, I had done everything the devil told me to do and that I would perform before hundreds and thousands of people with little or no clothes on. Was I saying that although I'm now saved and living for the Lord, I had nothing to say to God's people about how good He was? The devil was still trying to make me ashamed of my past.

Then AND *Now*

As time progressed, I continued receiving word after word that God was calling me into ministry to preach His word. However, I did not want to hear that. So I allowed two more years to go by. Then at work one day, I heard someone said loudly, "Bonnie." I turned around and saw no one. Then and there the Holy Ghost began to speak: "Will you obey me, my child? Will you? Will you give me that total yes I am looking for?"

I was so broken until I freely said, "Yes, Lord. Yes, Lord." It was then that I called my pastor, Apostle Miles, and told him that the Lord had called me to preach his Word and I had run from him for two years. I informed him that I was now ready to obey God.

Apostle Miles afforded me the opportunity to preach my first message; its title was "Do You Know Your Call in God?" God began to give me different gifts – including prophecy, interpretation, discernment of spirit and intercessory prayer. I began to yield to God for Him to use me fully for his glory. As a result of wholly yielding to God, I joined the following auxiliaries/departments at IGC: supervisor of the prayer partners department, encouraging people over the phone; choir; prayer band; nurses department; prison ministry; and nursery staff. I also assisted in many weddings and special events at the church. As I continued obeying God, doors opened for me to conduct revivals in many locations: Pontiac, Michigan; Queens, Brooklyn and Manhattan, New York; Greenville, North Carolina; Norfolk, Virginia; and Bridgeport, Connecticut.

Elder Robert and Sister Eazelle invited me, Dean, Ron and Doris to take part in a forty-day and -night fast with them. Elder Hodges said God was going to break some yokes in our lives. We set out on this fast to seek the Lord. On the twenty-sixth day, we broke the fast because Doris got sick and we all felt that the Lord had done what He said He

42

would do. We received a breakthrough in our marriage, our finances, our body and our soul. It was indeed God's will for us to go on this fast. Things began to look up for us. We got a car and an old truck, although they were so loud that whenever we pulled up in our driveway, the neighbors would come out and tell us not to park our cars there anymore because the sound was causing his baby to wake up.

After Dad Poole became sick, we were able to drive Mother Poole to church all the time. I can remember putting cardboard on the car floor to keep Mother Poole's feet from touching the ground. The muffler was so loud that it sounded like a big truck. As we would drive, we would run and pick up a muffler if we saw one, and often, the muffler would be on the other side of the expressway. As my husband ran across the expressway to get the muffler, I would be praying that he get the muffler so that he could put it on our car. Dean would find old cars and fix them up for us to drive and sell. He was a mechanic by trade and was able to take apart and put together cars. On one of our cars, the roof was out and water would come inside the car when it rained.

One day Apostle Miles called and asked Dean to meet him at the dealership to drop off his car. After they dropped off the car, Pastor Miles got in our car, and it began to rain. Pastor Miles had an umbrella, which he opened up to keep the rain off him. As he got out of the car, he told Dean, "Son, the Lord is going to bless you."

Matthew 25:21 affirms: *His lord said unto him, Well done, thou good and faithful servant: thou has been faithful over a few things, I will make thee ruler over many things: enter thou into the joy of thy lord.* We realized we had to work with what we had for God to bless us more. It was hard for me because I was used to more – much more. But I loved God more and wanted to be saved, and I was thankful to have a husband who loved me for who I was and never physically hurt me.

Dean went from job to job until he was employed at Church's Lumber Yard. After we came off our fast, Doris and I both found out we were pregnant. I was blessed because I had been trying to have a baby for some time and couldn't. I wanted a baby so badly that by faith I wore maternity clothes for four months. I even looked pregnant. People would ask, "When is the baby due?"

Also after the fast, we bought a new 1987 Nova. We were happy we no longer had to put mufflers on cars. However, during my pregnancy, our gas was turned off for one year and three months. We were forced to stay in one room of our house to get heat. We borrowed a hot plate to cook on. We borrowed a heater to keep the room warm. During this time, I also used the hot plate to heat water for baths. But the heated water would get cold by the time the next pot of water was heated. We even had delegates from Maryland, North Carolina and Curacao Island staying in our home for the convention during that period. The delegates started taking cold showers, and I prepared large meals on the hotplate. My baby was one month old then.

SEVEN

Tell It Like It Is

Don't Be Ashamed of Your Past

At this point in our lives, we were being blessed and truly forgiven for and freed from our past. In 2 Corinthians 5:17, 18, it states: *"Therefore if any man be in Christ, he is a new creature: old things are passed away; behold, all things are become new. And all things are of God, who hath reconciled us to himself by Jesus Christ, and hath given to us the ministry of reconciliation."* John 8:36 says: *"If the son therefore shall make you free, ye shall be free indeed."*

When Jesus forgives us of our past, He forgives us and He forgets it. So why can't we let it go? When we continue to hold onto our past, we cannot move into our future. I couldn't let it go. Later I knew I needed to let go of my past to experience all that God had planned for our lives.

For a long time I wouldn't talk about what God delivered me from until God released me to share it. My past was so bad I didn't want anyone to know about it. However,

God let me know that my past would bring deliverance to a lot of people. This book is all God's doing and none of mine. My family didn't even know about all of my past. God has released me to tell it and not to be ashamed because I used to be very ashamed of it.

Even the woman who drew water in Samaria had to tell her testimony. *"Come, see a man, which told me all things that ever I did: is not this the Christ?"* (John 4:29). Don't be ashamed of your past. Jesus told her to go and call her husband, and she said, I have no husband. Then Jesus said for thou hast five husbands, and he whom thou now hast is not thy husband.

So if you have been suffering as a Christian concerning your past, get up and shake the dust off of you, and don't be ashamed. Glorify God on your behalf because He has given you a testimony to be a witness to someone He will bring into your life. God will use everything we go through for His glory. Heed Psalm 31:1: *"In thee, O Lord, do I put my trust; let me never be ashamed: deliver me in thy righteousness."*

David was ashamed of his past at one time. But it came to pass that David cried out to God for help. David said, "Let me not be ashamed, for I called upon thee. I will testify before many and not be ashamed, for the Lord will help me."

I felt like David at one point. I needed God to help me because I didn't want to tell any of my testimony. I can remember when I first got saved and the saints would ask me what God delivered me from. I would say, "What difference does it make, as long as I am saved now." Thank God for that. We must be careful not to dwell on and talk about a person's past. We could wound that person. The Bible tells us to watch how we build on another person's foundation unless a worse thing happens unto us. He who is without sin cast the first stone. Jesus said we all have sinned and come short of the glory of God.

Tell It Like It Is

I have been saved and filled with his precious Holy Ghost for twenty-one years, and God just recently released me within the last three to four years to tell some parts of my life and from where He brought me. He wants me to tell how He had a plan for my life that I didn't know anything about. Thank God. Hallelujah.

God has given many of His people to share their testimonies, and they're ashamed. However, God will give you how much to share and what to say in that very same hour concerning your past. Remember, the Holy Ghost is not going to let you say something that will make you ashamed. Jesus said if you are ashamed of Him and where He brought you from, He will be ashamed when you come before His father. Tell your testimony. Tell it. Tell it. Now that God has released me to share my testimony, don't look at me from whence I came because you are really looking at a miracle. Remember, this is all God's doing because His hand was on my life all along.

I remember a sister getting saved and trying to share her testimony. Her past was so bad to some people that they began talking about her and would not let her forget her past. She went to different people and told them what God had saved her from. The news spread quickly, and her past was spread around until she became confused and bound. She was so bound that it was difficult for her to be fully delivered.

You're Not Alone

We all have faults and secrets. We have not told everything concerning us. Let us therefore pray for one another and love one another instead of trying to find out what a person was delivered from and thinking about other people's pasts. Instead, let's look at the God in that person. God will raise that very one up right before our eyes.

Then AND *Now*

Even though I was so ashamed and had asked God to give me something else to tell people instead of saying God delivered me from dancing and living a life of hell, God released me and said, "Tell it. Tell it, my child." We must realize that sin is sin, and God hates it all. So often we feel that one sin is worse than another. However, that's how man looks at it – not God. God died for us all, and He loves us all. Psalm 139:17, 18 says: *"How precious also are thy thoughts unto me, O God! how great is the sum of them! If I should count them, they are more in number than the sand: when I awake, I am still with thee."*

God loves us so much that He doesn't think about what we used to do. God thinks about you so much that His thoughts toward you cannot be numbered. Jeremiah 29:11 declares, *"For I know the thoughts that I think toward you, saith the Lord, thoughts of peace, and not of evil, to give you an expected end."* Your past means nothing to God. That's why He gave His Son, His only begotten Son, and who the Son set free is free indeed.

EIGHT

$\mathcal{V}$ISIONS $\mathcal{F}$ROM THE $\mathcal{L}$ORD

During my twenty-one years of salvation, God has given me numerous visions and dreams. They have made me so very thankful I made the decision, as well as frightened by what would have happened had I not. Joel 2:28 says, *"And it shall come to pass afterward, that I will pour out my spirit upon all flesh; and your sons and your daughters shall prophesy, your old men shall dream dreams, your young men shall see visions."* This is stated again in Acts 2:17: *"And it shall come to pass in the last days, saith God, I will pour out my Spirit upon all flesh: and your sons and your daughters shall prophesy, and your young men shall see visions, and your old men shall dream dreams."*

When I first got saved, time after time, God would show me an open vision as well as a dream. The first vision I saw was a cross that appeared in my window. It was then that I heard God say, "This is I." The year was 1983.

As I matured in the Lord, I remember lying in bed one night and, slipping in and out of sleep in the spirit, seeing my bed rising up toward heaven. Once I made it to heaven, there was a long line of people standing there. As I walked down the line, I saw different men and women from the Bible. I was so happy. It was so bright; light was everywhere. I began to follow others who were going down the line.

I saw the three Hebrew boys: Shadrach, Meshach and Abednego. I told them they blessed my soul when I read how they were cast into the fiery furnace and would not serve or worship the golden image Nebuchadnezzar had set up. I told them I loved it when they said, *"Our God whom we serve is able to deliver us from the burning fiery furnace, and He will deliver us out of thine hand, O king. But if not, be it known unto thee, O king, that we will not serve thy gods, nor worship the golden image which thou hast set up"* (Daniel 3: 17, 18). I told them I was impressed with their faith.

I continued down the line and saw Daniel in the lions' den. I told Daniel I was impressed with the way he stood up to the lions and was not afraid. I told him I liked how he said, *"My God hath sent his angel, and hath shut the lions' mouths, that they have not hurt me"* (Daniel 6:22). I said, "Daniel, I love your story. It blessed my soul."

As I continued down the line, I screamed out for Moses, for I had to see him. As I looked down the line, I saw a hand go up and heard Moses say, "Here am I." He was white as snow, and his hair was long and white as could be. Once I reached him, I began crying as I told him what a man of God he was. I wondered how he was patient with the children of Israel, even though they caused him hurt and pain many times over, and how he continued praying for God not to kill them. I said to Moses, "That was a bad rod you had in your hand. I liked it when you said, *'Fear ye not, stand still, and see the salvation of the Lord … for the Egyptians whom ye have seen to day ye shall see them again no more for ever. The Lord shall fight for you, and ye shall hold your peace'* (Exodus 14:13, 14). You took the rod, Moses, and stretched out your hand over the Red Sea, it divided on both sides, and the children of Israel went through on dry ground. Moses, I enjoyed reading about all the miracles God brought to the children of Israel. You are a mighty man of God."

I told him I was looking for my mom and dad and asked if he had seen them. He said, "Go down to the left side, and you will find them." As I got there, I said, "Mom, Dad, this is me, Bonnie. Hey, I made it." I began hugging and embracing them. Crying, I asked, "Where are Pastor Hyman and my sister, First Lady White?" Mom said, "I just saw them go up to your mansion. Bonnie, stop back by on the way out." I said, "On the way out? I am not going anywhere." I looked back at mom, and she said nothing. She simply smiled.

When I reached my mansion, I said hi to my sweet sister and Pastor Hyman. I said, "I made it. Yes! Yes! Yes!" As I said that, I felt myself slipping back, and I screamed and said, "Wait a minute. Where is Jesus, the One Who died for me?" As I turned around, I felt someone touch me on the shoulder. I looked, and it was Jesus. I bowed down and worshipped Him and said, "Thank you, Jesus, for saving me. Thank you, Jesus, for keeping me. Thank you, Jesus, for delivering me. Thank you, Jesus, for not leaving me." I held his legs, and when I looked up to see his face, he turned and said, "Go back now." I began to look around, and next thing I knew, I was back home in my bed. I wanted to go back to God, but I could not get back into the vision. I began praising the Lord, crying and wishing I were in heaven.

My next vision occurred years later. This time, God took me into hell. I saw nothing but blackness as far as I could see. I looked, and behold, Jesus appeared and said to me, "Look and follow me." I looked and began to see people in nothing but blackness. As we walked, Jesus said, "See those people over there, I gave them chance after chance to get it right, but they did not listen to my warnings. People in this room did not make it in. There are preachers in this room who led My people astray."

Then I looked deep, deep down and saw all kinds of fires burning. I didn't say a word. I just looked. I saw that the fire was so high it seemed as if I could feel it. I saw all kinds of people burning, with fire coming out of their ears, mouths, eyes and noses. Their skin was brown. I kept looking back as they screamed and cried out. Then we came to a dark place, and I saw people with their hands up saying, "Help, help, help, please!" I looked, and there I saw one of my friends. I began to say in my spirit, "What are you doing here? We walked together and prayed together." With a low voice, she said, "Help me, Bonnie. Help me."

What I saw was frightening, and I was ready to go. Then Jesus said, "Many of my people will die and surely go to hell." After that, Jesus began ministering to me.

Another time while in the spirit, Jesus showed me a huge clock. The time displayed was 11:57. Jesus said, "Time is winding up, and it is getting later in the hour. Tell my people to repent, truly repent. I am coming soon, and I am coming back for a church that is ready – not getting ready, but ready. It is time out for show and fame. Time is winding up. Repent. Repent. Truly turn to me and repent. I am coming soon."

In yet another vision, I was suspended between heaven and earth, and Jesus was dipping me up and down in a big river. The last time he dipped me, the water was as gold as gold could be. Jesus said to me: "I am getting you ready for a great work that I have in store for you to do. You must be ready for this new level that I'm taking you to."

In my next vision, I saw a long, white ladder coming down from heaven. Jesus said, "Do you see those people on those steps?" I said, "Yes." Jesus said, "The ones at the bottom who keep getting up and falling back down are weighed down with the cares of this world. They will never make it in. The ones in the middle have made it thus far. However, they too have weights and cares and are all bound up. They will stay right there. Look at the ones at the top. They have hallelujah signs. They made it in, and they are holding the victory signs."

Another time while in the spirit, God said to me, "Look at your hands." I looked, and both my hands were on fire. God said He had put fire in my hands. He told me to use my hands.

On another occasion, Jesus said, "Open your bosom." As I obeyed, money from heaven began falling into my bosom. Jesus said, "Into your house I will fill, and in wealth you will be filled, and my blessing shall overtake you."

Another instance while deep in the spirit, I saw Jesus on the water. He took my hand and said, "Come." I held his hand tight, and I looked and said, "Jesus is standing on water." Then I looked down at my feet, and I too was standing on water. When I looked at the water, I began to go down, and Jesus said, "Come." As I kept my eyes on Jesus, I continued toward him. He then said, "As long as you keep your eyes on me, nothing shall be impossible for you. You can speak to the mountain, and it has to move. I will not withhold anything from you."

Once while in the spirit, God showed me my husband and three of my daughters standing on the floor, money raining down on us from heaven. So much money fell that it covered us all up to our necks. We all began to play in the money. Then God said, "Your blessings shall overtake you, and wealth shall overtake you. You will have so much money until you won't have room enough to receive it. Every time you turn around, I will keep blessing you."

Then AND *Now*

Another time, I asked God to show me my nine babies that I had lost during miscarriages. One night while my family and I were praying, God took me into the spirit, and I looked on the wall, and behold, there were all nine of my unborn children. I looked at the first one, and he said, "Mommy." I gave him a big hug. I looked at the second one, and he said, "Mommy," and I gave him a big hug. I looked at the third one, and he said, "Mommy," and I gave him a big hug. I began crying very hard and screaming out and saying, "Lord, show them to my husband. Lord, show them to the girls. As this was my vision, they were unable to see them.

The fourth baby said, "Mommy," and I looked at her and gave her a big hug. Then the fifth one said, "Mommy," and I gave her a big hug. The sixth one said, "Mommy," and I gave her a big hug. The seventh one said, "Mommy," and I looked at her and gave her a bug hug. I looked at the eighth one, and she said, "Mommy," and I gave her a big hug. I looked at the ninth one, and she said, "Mommy," and I gave her a big hug. She looked just like one of our daughters we have now. God allowed me to see all nine babies. But not only did He let me see them, He allowed me to hug each one and let each baby call me Mommy. I was screaming, crying, jumping, laughing and thanking God for the vision.

Before the vision, I didn't know what sex my unborn babies were. Afterward, I knew the first three were boys and the next six were girls. Thank you, Jesus, for that vision!

God allowed me to see all nine babies one other time. That time, they were all in a room with white on, and they appeared to be working or something. I just looked at them.

NINE

My *B*ABIES

Although I had lost nine babies, the Lord blessed my husband and me with four daughters: Tawana, Kenyatta, Chantel and LaChisa. Girls, I love you all! Even then, the devil was still trying to destroy us. He tried to use three of our girls. From the time she was a baby, Kenyatta loved the "Barney" show. As soon as she heard the theme song from "Barney" (*I love you. You love me. We're one happy family. With a great big hug and a kiss from me to you, won't you say you love me too?*), she would go to the television and sit until the show ended.

When she was three years old, the "Barney" show came to the Northland Mall nearby. At that time, I had a day care center (Bonnie's Christian Day Care Center), with eight to ten children enrolled. I took all my children to the mall to see Barney. The television news channels were there filming. They especially wanted to talk to the children who had a special interest in Barney. Kenyatta was one of those children.

That night, she was on the local news. The television crew showed her at Barney's show in the mall. They want-

Then AND *Now*

Kenyatta Baker, 3, cuddles figures of Barney while watching one of his videos. Marlon Hammons, 13 months, has other interests. *The Detroit News*, 1992.

ed to come to our home to interview her for the show, and we gave them permission to do so. The next day, Kenyatta's interview was in the local newspaper. She was now on her way to the big screen. They wanted us to bring her to New York to interview her and to do a taping of her on the show. At that time, she was in first grade, and we were told there would be several weeks of taping and she would receive on-the-road tutoring instead of going to school.

At first, this sounded good and exciting. I asked my sister-in-law Doris if she would go with me to New York, as my husband had just gotten a job at Chrysler and wasn't able to go. Doris said she would go. However, as I began to think about it, I became uneasy in my spirit. The Holy Ghost began dealing with me, and I quickly changed my mind and decided not to go. The people from the show were waiting for me to get back with them. They had taken care of the hotel and everything.

But just in time, God let me see that the devil was trying to plant that same spirit into my child – big city, big money! I said no. They could not believe this because there were so many people who wanted to bring their children to be a part of the "Barney" show. I took the attitude that we would wait on God to bless us, as Habakkuk 2:3 states: *"For the vision is yet for an appointed time, but at the end it shall speak, and not lie: though it tarry, wait for it; because it will surely come, it will not tarry."*

After that, my two baby daughters, Chantel and LaChisa, went to Detroit to audition for the production of "The Wizard of Oz." About four hundred to six hundred children were there to audition for the show. Wouldn't you know it, my daughters were chosen to perform in "The Wizard of Oz." Out of 600 children auditioning, they were the only two chosen. We attended the show. We were allowed in the dressing room, and we met the entire cast. We also received front-row seats. They played munchkins, and the people in charge wanted them to travel with the show. They too would have been tutored while on the road. This sounded good.

But again, I saw a trap that the devil had set. This would have taken us away from church. It would again have been big city, big money! Again, the devil tried to destroy us. It was a trap to take our minds off Jesus. But we didn't give the devil a chance. Again, we waited on God to bless us, as Psalm 62:5 instructs: *"My soul, wait thou only upon God; for my expectation is from him."*

A few more years of waiting, and it came – the blessing of the Lord – because we waited and did not settle for anything. The Lord is blessing Tawana. She is finishing school this year, and she has her driver's license. Thank God. Glory to God. Praise His holy name.

Chantel and LaChisa

TEN

You Can Make It

Going Through

No matter what you are going through, know that you too will make it with God's help, and you will feel peace and receive many blessings from God. As John 16:33 states: *"These things I have spoken unto you, that in me ye might have peace. In the world ye shall have tribulation: but be of good cheer; I have overcome the world."*

When the Lord saved me, I was going through really bad. But several people helped me in different areas of my life. I had no money with which to pay my bills, nor did I have money to buy food or gas for my new 1980 Lincoln. One night at church, Apostle Miles was praying for everyone. When he got to me, he said, "Daughter, God said He is going to bless you. I see you going through. If I have, you will have also. If I eat, you will too." That really blessed my soul because the church was so large that I didn't know Apostle Miles knew me. My neighbors, Marlene and

Matthew, became my very best friends. They often would invite me over for dinner. They began asking me if I wanted to ride to church with them. I said yes because I didn't have money for gas. This was a blessing. My close friend gave me all kinds of dresses and shoes. She would cook cakes (which I loved eating). Mother Poole began helping me. I began selling things in my house so I would have money.

After I married Dean, we really started going through one thing after another. I felt like Job. I like what Job said in Job 14:14: *"If a man die, shall he live again? All the days of my appointed time will I wait, till my change come."* Often it's good to go through when you think about the blessings behind it. It says in 1 Peter 4:12, 13: *"Beloved, think it not strange concerning the fiery trial which is to try you, as though some strange thing happened unto you: But rejoice, inasmuch as ye are partakers of Christ's sufferings; that, when his glory shall be revealed, ye may be glad also with exceeding joy."* Like Job, the devil took me down to nothing. Like Job, I held on to God's hand and would not let go until He blessed me.

As we continued to go through, I would say my favorite Scripture, Psalm 23:1, over and over: *"The Lord is my shepherd; I shall not want."* Slowly, God began to bring us out. The devil began fighting me in my body with different sicknesses. I remember when I was in a deep trial. That Christmas I became really sick and had chest pains. My husband took me to the emergency room, and I went straight back. I was immediately hooked up to many machines, including the IV machine. Several tests were run. I wasn't aware that I was slipping in and out. I was placed on life support.

My husband was called in and told that I was having a heart attack and I had to be admitted to the hospital. While he and the girls were in my hospital room, I lost consciousness again. When I opened my eyes, I was standing above the bed, and I looked down and said, "That is me, and I'm dead." I looked around the room and saw my husband, the girls and all the doctors. I saw them beating me in the chest with several devices, counting 1-2-3, then hitting me again. My husband and the girls looked very hurt. They were crying. They said I was out four to five minutes.

When I opened my eyes, I was back in the bed, and I heard, "We have a heartbeat now." My family went home, and I stayed in the hospital. The girls later told me that they had prayed for about forty-five minutes. They said Dean prayed, "Lord, don't let her die. Please, Lord, don't let her die." I asked one of the girls why she thought her daddy was praying and crying so hard for the Lord to keep me. She said, "You know, Mommy, so you could come back home and cook and clean up the house and stuff." I made it out, and everything was okay. Glory to God.

Coming Out

In 1 Peter 5:10, the Bible says, *"But the God of all grace, who hath called us unto his eternal glory by Christ Jesus, after that ye have suffered a while, make you perfect, stablish, strengthen, settle you."*

As God has the power to lift us up and strengthen us, we began coming out. God began to bless us after coming off of that twenty-six day and -night fast. We could see the breaking of day. Coming out is joy. Coming out is freedom. Coming out is happiness. Coming out is everything you need.

I found out you have to call the things that be not as though they were. So I asked for it. I had claimed it and named it and was looking for it. We had been in that storm of going through long enough. I began to cry out to God during that fast, and as a result, God freed my mind, my spirit and my soul. When praises go up, blessings come down. I had to praise him for it. I was like a woman in labor. She has to carry her baby for nine months, during which she goes through three stages, or trimesters, and the baby comes in the third stage. God let me know that I was still in the first stage and I had to go to the second and third stages. He also let me know that when I reached the third stage, I would come out.

God let me know I had to push a little more, I had to grow a little more. When I pushed, the baby (blessings) would come. God said when I came out, I would have the full reward – all the things He had promised me and all the things I had been waiting on. I remember the last word Apostle Miles said to me that Tuesday night before he went to be with God: "Bonnie, I don't see anything but victory, nothing but victory." He was right. God did bring us out, and it was nothing but total victory. We got all the promises, all the words, all the prophecies, everything. We got it. We came out on top. Thank God! Hallelujah!

ELEVEN

ℛECEIVING THE ℬLESSINGS

Walking Into the Blessings

In 1993, we began walking into our blessing. My husband was going to go on a trip with Apostle Miles to London, Holland and Africa. But the down payment was between three thousand and four thousand dollars, and we didn't have the money. The deadline was fast-approaching, and we were wondering where we would get the money for the trip. My husband really wanted to go. The day arrived when all monies were due, and we still didn't have it, so my husband came home on his lunch hour and was sad. We decided to call Pastor Miles and ask him to lend us the money. As my husband picked up the phone to call, I said, "Wait. Let me check the mail." There was a lot of mail, and I said, "Maybe there is a check in the mail." I began opening the mail and thought I saw a check. I said, "Dean, look at this and see if this is a check." He looked at it while I continued sifting through the other mail.

He said, "This is a check." I said, "For that amount?" He said, "Yes." As we continued opening the mail and praising and thanking God, I saw another check. In all, we opened seven checks. I had applied for my unemployment from my job, and I had received it. That check totaled thirteen weeks' pay. We had enough money to pay all the bills and for him to go on the trip and take about five thousand dollars with him to Africa. My husband, I and the children in my day care center began praising God for making a way.

The blessings began that day and continued flowing. For eight years, I waited for the settlement from a lawsuit I had filed. I received my settlement at that time. My workers' compensation check arrived too. Money started flowing from everywhere. The Lord was truly blessing us. We were able to buy a new van, something we had been wanting for quite some time.

Deuteronomy 28:2 says, *"And all these blessings shall come on thee, and overtake thee, if thou shalt hearken unto the voice of the Lord thy God."*

Deuteronomy 28:12 says, *"The Lord shall open unto thee his good treasure, the heaven to give the rain unto thy land in his season, and to bless all the work of thine hand: and thou shalt lend unto many nations, and thou shalt not borrow."*

We were seeking the Lord for the trip, fasting and praying for God to make a way, as Matthew 6:33 says: *"But seek ye first the kingdom of God, and his righteousness; and all these things shall be added unto you."* God will not hold anything from you if you put Him first because he wants us to have the best and not to want for anything. After my husband returned from Africa with Pastor Miles, he told me he wanted to start a business. I asked, "What do you mean?" He said he wanted to start a vending business. He informed me that he had met a man at Church's Lumber Yard that had several vending machines. He allowed Dean to get one without having to pay for it at that time because God had given him favor. Shortly after, he obtained his second machine. God began to bless him, and soon he had ten machines that brought in between three thousand and four thousand dollars per week. We were on our way.

I gave up the day care center because I was responsible for managing the money from Dean's vending business and taking it to the bank because Dean had gotten a job at Chrysler Corp. He had applied for that job while working at Church's Lumber Yard. Chrysler called him in, and he passed a test. But when he took the medical examination, they found traces of blood in his urine. They told him he had to go to the doctor so they could clear that up. But weeks went by and it was not cleared up. By that time, everyone else who had taken the test with him had received his assignment.

Dean had two more chances to go back to the doctor to have this condition cleared up. We called Pastor Miles, others at our church, Pastor Hyman, and my sister and my brother-in-law in North Carolina to pray with us. It seemed that the blood in his urine just would not clear up. God began giving him favor with the nurses at the desk. The second time he did not pass the blood urine test, the nurses told him to walk outside and come back in as if he had never been there. They performed the test again and again, but he did not pass the test. The nurse told him to go out and come back in one more time. This was the fourth test, and still he did not pass it.

Then the nurse told him to go home and come back sometime in the next two weeks. She said they would note that this was the second time he had been in. In the midst of all that, he had to go into the hospital to see if the doctors could stop the small trace of blood in his urine. After praying and fasting, he was to take the test for the fifth time. Three months had passed, and he had received word after word that the job was his and that God was going to promote him on the job. We were praying and believing God. To our surprise, when he took the test on the fifth try, he still did not pass. However, the doctor passed him anyway, and he got the job a few days later.

Proverbs 12:2 says, *"A good man obtaineth favour of the Lord: but a man of wicked devices will he condemn."* God truly had given him favor in all of this. Praise be unto our Lord and Savior. There was much praying, fasting, favor and believing God taking place for this.

He has been there for ten years now and will be coming out soon because of the blessing of God. God really began to bless us. For my birthday, my husband bought me a brand new 1996 Sable. We were walking in the blessings of the Lord. We were paying our tithes and giving every time anyone called for an offering. We began believing God for everything we wanted.

God can open doors that no man can open, and He can close doors that no man can close. But whatever the situation, Philippians 4:19 assures us that He will provide for our needs: *"But my God shall supply all your need according to his riches in glory by Christ Jesus."* It is nothing for God to change an impossible situation for you only if you believe. God will make the impossible things possible because all things are possible with God.

We no longer had to pick up Mother Poole in a worn-out car. She even would say, "Baby, the Lord is not through blessing you." We began to receive different words and prophesy about how the Lord was going to bless us and that we were going to be millionaires. We received word after word, and we can say today that we are walking in the blessings of the Lord. The Lord has truly blessed us.

Unfortunately, my mother and father did not have a chance to share the blessings of the Lord with me. I wanted them to see the blessings because they saw all that the devil had given me and they saw me lose it all.

I lost my dad in 1994. Eight months later, I lost my mom. I know my mother was a praying woman of God and could see a lot of things in the spirit. The Lord walked with her when she was a child. He appeared to her in the form of a big white dog that would take her from camp to camp. She would see many different visions from the Lord. Just before she died, she would tell my sister and Pastor Hyman what the Lord was showing her. She said she saw her mother, Jesus, her brother and others calling her to come home. She often would say, "I am going home."

Two weeks before she died, she wanted to see each of her children. All her children who lived in Greenville and her adopted daughter, Pastor Hyman, had the opportunity to see her. She ministered to her children as they went in to see her. She talked to the four of us who were out of town on the phone. Mama was giving all her children a heavy word from the lord. She wanted all of us to be saved, and to get along with and love one another.

When I called her, she began praying for me and said, "God, bless my Bonnie." She prayed so hard and long until God took her in the spirit and she said, "God is going to let you have two more children, and they are going to look like twins. Name one after Dean and one after Jack," one after my husband's side of the family and one after my side. She said, "God is going to bless you and Dean real good."

I began to cry, and she would not hang up the phone. She began to tell me how much she loved me. That was a sad moment for me. After we hung up the phone, I cried and wiped my eyes. After a few days, I fell on my knees and began to say to God, "I release her, God. You can take her now." My sister, Sister White, had been telling all of us to release her and let her go.

Then AND *Now*

Two weeks later, my mother went home to be with the Lord. There was a deep void in my life. I missed my mother so much, and for months, I felt like I could not get over her being gone. All my brothers and sisters were saying how they would dream about daddy and mama. I never did. I told my sister I missed mama, and she said she did too. She also said that to be absent from the body is to be present with the Lord. She said mama had suffered a lot and never complained about the pain she encountered. She told me to rejoice and be glad that mama was with God.

But I could not rejoice because I wanted her to be with us. Then I began to pray to God. I said, "Lord, fill this void." I still wanted my mother. I asked God to give me another mother. Mother Mary Jordan-Meeks (at that time, her name was Jordan) had traveled with me out of town on different revivals. The Lord spoke to me and said, "I have given you another mother." I said, "Who? Mother Jordan?" The Lord said, "Yes."

I told Mother Jordan what the Lord had said, and she became my new mom and still is to this day. Her biological children accepted me as their new sister. Within the next ten months, my two other daughters came, and people asked if they were twins because they looked alike, just like my mother said. Everything she told me has come to pass.

I still miss dad and mom today, and although my parents did not get a chance to witness our blessings, my mother knew the Lord was going to bless me and Dean real good. Many others told us the same thing, and we are now walking in those blessings.

Seasons of Blessings

Ecclesiastes 3:1 says, *"To every thing there is a season, and a time to every purpose under the heaven."* And this was the time we began to experience seasons of blessings. Every time we turned around, we were being blessed.

Countless Scriptures promise these blessings we were receiving. Leviticus 25:21 says, *"Then will I command my blessing upon you in the sixth year, and it shall bring forth fruit for three years."* In Genesis 22:17 it says, *"That in blessing I will bless thee, and in multiplying I will multiply thy seed as the stars of the heaven, and as the sand which is upon the sea shore; and thy seed shall possess the gate of his enemies."*

While weeping may endure for a night, joy comes in the morning. One thousand years is like one day to God, and it's morning time to God, and this is your morning to be blessed. Nobody can bless you like Jesus can. The Word tells us that the blessing of the Lord maketh rich and addeth no sorrow with it. He shall receive the blessings from the Lord and righteousness from the God of his salvation. In this latter day, did not God say, "I will put out a blessing upon my people"?

Ezekiel 34:26 says, *"And I will make them and the places round about my hill a blessing; and I will cause the shower to come down in his season; there shall be showers of blessing."* God will open the windows of heaven and pour out blessings onto you that there shall not be room enough to receive them.

That is what God did for us. We received the season of blessings.

The blessing of the Lord rests upon His people, as stated in Proverbs 10:6: *"Blessings are upon the head of the just: but violence covereth the mouth of the wicked."* Because we were the just, God began to take us into the season of blessings.

We had lived at the old house for fourteen years and wanted to move into something bigger. The house on

Hartwell had been a blessing from God. At that time, we bought it for twenty-two thousand dollars. We began believing God for a bigger house, and we began to look for one. We looked at house after house until we found the one God had for us. We knew that for us to get this house was God's doing. We encountered many challenges trying to sell the house we had lived in previously. We did find a buyer for our home, but six weeks later, we learned he wasn't approved.

My sister walked us through disappointment after disappointment, house after house. She said the Lord said this one was ours. She began to pray with us and to encourage us. The mortgage company could not get the lender to approve this loan. At first, they wanted twenty percent down. My sister said we would not have to put that much down. I was getting very discouraged. My husband said he would not look at another house if we didn't get this one.

But God gave me favor with Ms. Winn, president of Jireh Financial Mortgage Co. She told me I could be a good loan officer because I was a good salesperson. I did not want to be a loan officer; I just wanted my loan to be approved. My sister kept me encouraged. I called her one day crying and saying they were going to put the house back on the market if we didn't get a final approval to close on this deal. I asked her to lend us the money until we sold our old house.

Then she called me one day and said: "God said this is your house. I want you to dress up, go to the office and tell the president of the company to call the lender and tell them thus saith the Lord." I didn't go at that time. It was getting close to the time when we would lose our deposit of eight thousand dollars. We were approved upon a final condition. Time passed, and we continued to try to sell our house. Everything seemed to be going wrong. All the faith

I once had was being tested. I was frustrated and exhausted from all of this.

My sister called again and said, "God is going to do it. Get dressed up, go into the office, talk to the president of the mortgage company, and tell her you can only put down five percent and tell her God said it was in her hands. Tell her God said for her to call the lender and get the final approval on this deal." After I hung up from talking to her, I called my Pastor Marvin Miles, crying, telling him all about this.

All he said was, "It's got to happen. It's done." I wanted a word from the Lord, and that is all he said. We hung up, and after a while, that which Pastor Miles and my sister said got into my spirit. I got up, got sugar sharp (dressed up) and went into the office.

With Holy Ghost boldness, I told my boss everything my sister told me to tell her. I told her that God said the outcome was in her hands and that God was going to use her. I thought about what Pastor had said, "It's got to happen." Ms. Winn got on the speaker phone and called the lender. She told the lender everything I told her to say. I whispered "Favor, Lord, favor." The lender put us on hold and said, "I will be right back." The underwriter was a friend of the president of the mortgage company. Before we hung up the phone, we asked her to sign off on this deal. The boss informed her that I was listening to the conversation. I was so nervous, yet I believed God. When the lender returned to the phone, she said, "I am not supposed to do this, but I am going to sign off on this deal so that the Bakers can close."

My heart almost dropped. While the lender was on the phone, I began saying, "Thank you, Jesus. Glory to God." We hung up, and the other people in the office began rejoicing with me because they knew that this file was a dif-

71

ficult one. In the office, they called it the Baker file, the longest and hardest deal they ever had. We closed on the house on March 31, 2000, the house with which God blessed us. We put down five percent on the new house, and the underwriter gave us everything we asked for. After we closed on our house, we found a buyer for our house on Hartwell Street in Detroit.

After that I went on to became a loan officer. I went to school to become a loan officer and failed the first two tests, but they allowed me to write up different deals to learn how to do the job so I could pass the test. Finally, I got my license and began to work as a loan officer. My first check was so good I began to like it. I thank Ms. Winn for giving me a chance in this business. I stayed there for about a year and a half before I moved to another company.

At the new company, I brought in all kinds of deals. One day I got a phone call from the president of the new company. He said, "We want you to be the district manager." I had been the executive senior loan officer, and I thought that was okay. I told him I would call him back because I had to talk to my husband as well as my Pastor.

My husband said, "Take the job." I still wanted to hear what Pastor had to say. He said the same thing. I didn't have to go to school for his position. God gave it to me. The only school I attended was "on-my-knees school," where I prayed to God. God has really blessed us all the way around in seasons of blessings.

Since getting the house, God has blessed us with a Mercedes Benz, a P.T. Cruiser, two trucks, a van and two boats. The blessings of the Lord were flowing. We have come a mighty long way. Thanks be to God!

TWELVE

DEAN, MY HUSBAND, MY BLESSING

One blessing I received in my life that is more awesome than can be described is my husband, Dean, my friend, my babies' daddy, the one God gave me, the one I love so very much, the one who went through things with me, the one who held me when I cried and told me, "It's going to be all right. I'm here." He is the one who has and does love me for who I am. He is the one who encouraged and continues to encourage me when I am sad. I know God gave me this man. We have been through a lot together, and now we are in the blessing of the Lord.

Together, we thank God for all that He has given us, past and future blessings. I look forward to growing old with this man and holding our grandchildren together. People look at us today and call us blessed. But they have no idea how blessed we truly are. They were not there when we went through time and again. They ask why we have so many cars. They were not there when my husband practically had to put a car together just so we had something to drive. They ask why I have so many clothes, suits and shoes. They were not there when I got saved and had only one dress I could wear. They comment on my hair being done all the time. They were not there when I could not afford to have my hair done and had to wear a wig. They wonder why I have a glass dinette set and white furniture in my house. They were not there when we had to sit on the floor in the living room and in the kitchen for many years. That is why we can say now that we are enjoying the blessings of the Lord. God has smiled on us.

Dean, thank you for being here for me and the girls. From my heart to your heart, my love for you will never die. I love you, I love you, I love you. I thank God that He had you waiting for me until I got saved. Dean, you were mine even before the foundation of the world. You were mine even when I was in my mother's womb. You were mine even before I said my first word. You were mine after all I went through – tasting death, thinking I was dead, being shot at, running, hiding and listening to the devil saying, "Just kill yourself." I could not die then because from the foundation, God had a plan for my life and, Dean, you were a part of that plan. I love you!

My Family

ABOUT THE AUTHOR

Bonnie Baker was born in Vredenburgh, Alabama, 45 miles from Selma, Alabama, where Dr. Martin Luther King Jr. led the famous march. She moved to Detroit in 1973.

The Lord saved her in 1982 and called her into ministry in 1985, and now she is totally sold out to God. God has blessed her with the gifts of intercessory prayer, discernment of spirits, prophecy and interpretation, laying on of hands, preaching and ministry of helps, among others. The Lord has used her to help many of His people through their Christian walk and to give them a NOW word from Him.

She married her husband Dean in 1983. She has four daughters: Tawana, Kenyatta, Chantel and LaChisa; and nine children in heaven (three sons and six daughters). She has one spiritual child and twelve godchildren.

She has received many visions and revelations from the Lord. God let her know that *Then and Now* will provide healing and deliverance while touching thousands. Also look for her upcoming books, *Surviving Your Worst Fears* and *Then and Now–Part II*.

Bonnie has had much success since coming to Michigan. Her goal was to be a nurse, but her life took a different direction as she became a great entertainer. Many times she was almost killed as a result of sin. She encountered many obstacles, but God brought her out.

The Lord blessed her and her husband financially after going through for many years. They currently own four businesses and plan to open three more soon. Bonnie is the district manager for a well-known mortgage company and a notary public. She lives by the Scriptures that say, God will bless you coming in and going out. He will make you the head and not the tail. Be blessed in the name of The Lord!

Author Contact
P.O. Box 74073
Romulus, MI 48174-0073